THE POWER OF GOOD HABITS

HOW TO CHANGE YOURSELF

IN EASY STEPS AND FEEL GREAT !

By Alex Canny

Table of Contents

COPYWRIGHT

The information presented in this report solely and fully represents the views of the author as of the date of publication. Any omission, or potential Misrepresentation of, any peoples or companies, is entirely unintentional. As a result of changing information, conditions or contexts, this author reserves the right to alter content at their sole discretion impunity. The report is for informational purposes only and while every attempt has been made to verify the information contained herein, the author, assumes no responsibility for errors, inaccuracies, and omissions. Each person has unique needs and this book cannot take these individual differences into account.

This e-book is copyright © 2019 by the Author with all rights reserved. It is illegal to copy, distribute, or create derivative works from this ebook in whole or in part. No part of this report may be reproduced or transmitted in any form whatsoever, electronic, or mechanical, including photocopying, recording, or by any informational storage or retrieval system without expressed written, dated and signed permission from the author.

INTRODUCTION

Part of living a healthy lifestyle is transforming your new knowledge, eating plan, exercise plan or inspiration into a daily habit. Teachers, bosses, medical professionals, life coaches, and just about every successful person stresses the importance of forming good habits, but have you ever wondered why habits are important?

You'll find here seven benefits to forming good habits and some practical tips to start creating new habits today.

Habits are who you are

What is a habit? A habit is something you do daily without thinking much about it. You probably have a habit of waking at a certain time, brushing your teeth a certain way, and perhaps calling your mom once a week on a Tuesday night. Habits become such a part of your routine that they become who you are. Want to be a different person? Just start a new habit!

You can change your habits

The nice thing about habits is that you can change them. Old habits may be hard to break it seems that the worst habits are the hardest to break but it is possible. If you want to start eating healthier, all you have to do is skip your morning donut until it becomes second nature to turn down pastries at breakfast.

Good habits allow you to reach your goals

If you wanted to become a marathon runner, you wouldn't just jump into the first marathon offered by your city. It takes months or years of training to become fit enough to compete in a marathon race. Step one of reaching any goal is establishing a daily habit. If you want a better job, you must start the daily habit of looking for work. If you want to be able to lift 300 pounds, you must start the daily habit of lifting weights.

Habits set a foundation for life

Since habits become you, the habits that you choose to follow set the tone for your entire life. If you have a habit of greeting your children with joy, you will become a joyful person. If you have a habit of eating a vegetable with every meal, you will become a healthy person.

Habits are step one of your life plan

If you have a life goal, it isn't the goal itself that will help you reach your dreams, it is the habits that you form and follow while you are trying to get there. Habits are the basic building blocks of reaching any goal or succeeding in any plan.

Habits eliminate wasted time

As humans, we tend to waste a lot of time. Most of us would rather not do anything difficult or challenging. However, if we create good habits, we become more efficient and this reduces how much time we waste.

Habits can replace motivation

We all have days when we just don't feel like working, exercising or eating well. But when these things are habits, they become second nature and we do them without thinking. When healthy eating becomes a habit, although you may eat one slice of cake today, you probably won't eat more and will go right back to making healthy choices tomorrow.

Easy ways to start new habits

Try these tips for implementing new, good habits in your life:

Create a behavior chain: Rather than the abstract goal of "I need to exercise daily," create an action chain that helps you get there, such as, "After I get home from work, I will change into exercise clothes, socialize for thirty minutes, and then go for a run." Research shows this kind of planning is more effective for creating healthy habits.

Don't fall off the wagon: When you are starting a new habit, little things can derail your effort before it becomes a habit. You can prevent this by finding out what causes you to want to quit and eliminating that trigger. You may also find ways to make it easier to settle in to your new habit. It could be as simple as changing into exercise clothes as soon as you walk in the door or removing junk food from the house.

Creating a foundation of healthy habits will benefit your life from today far into the future. This is not an impossible task and a few simple tricks can make the process much easier. Follow these simple strategies to get on track and see your life blossom.

CH. 1 THE POWER OF GOOD HABITS

Productivity is an important aspect of our daily lives. It is important to be productive in our work, in our personal and family lives. But how does a person become productive? The simple answer is by developing a chain of Good Habits.

What does it meant to be productive?

A lot of people have mistakenly linked up productivity with busyness at work or at any social activities. The busier a person gets, the more productive a person feels or thinks. However, as we are caught in these busy schedules, and in this fast- changing environment, we forget to set goals, and plan our lives. Being productive means you are able to accomplish your goals without having to sacrifice your passion, happiness, and personal growth.

Being busy is not always bad, however if you put too much effort on doing tasks that are not really important, you are leading a life of wastefulness. Some people have been successful in living productive lives, but a lot of people have shrunk from problems, stress, criticism, and discouragements. And these negativities in life can also affect our attitude toward work, family, and personal growth.

First and foremost, it is essential to slow down. For some people, slowing down means weakness, defeat, and limitation. However, for productive people, slowing down allows a person to be open to newer and better perspectives. When you slow down, you are able to reevaluate your mental wellbeing, allowing you to reassess your feelings, insights, and senses.

Secondly, it is important to contemplate on mistakes and learn from them. Mistakes should not be taken as failure; instead, mistakes should be taken as a road to success. A mistake allows a person to develop new solutions. Productive people know the value of learning from mistakes.

Thirdly, productive people make a list. Making a list is seems very simple and easy, but this habit is vital to accomplishing goals. It is easy to be overcame by tasks, schedules, and commitments, but creating a list would isolate distractions, and drives you to focus on progress. Simply write your things to be done early in the morning, and at the end of the day, you will know that you have been productive.

Fourth, time management should be implemented. We are now living in a world where there is so much distraction. Technological advancements contribute to ineffective time management. Social media, text messaging, and apps can definitely divide your time, and may cause you to be inefficient.

Lastly, believe in yourself and simplify your life. Believe that you can change, and you will, because you will have the motivation and the will to change. Simplifying your life keeps you from discontentment, envy, and stress. You can be more happy and satisfied.

CH. 2 HOW TO DEVELOP GOOD HABITS

Success is the result of little things done successfully over and over each day. An Olympic athlete does not win the race at the time of the race, but rather during the vigorous training. Therefore, success, in itself, is not an end goal to reach, but a series of good habits resulting in positive balanced growth in every area of life. However, most people have a difficult time with changing their habits. Here, you will find 3 simple steps that will help you develop any positive habit with ease.

❖ **Become aware of your habits.**

All progress starts with awareness first. If you want to improve your finances, you will first want to record every income and expenditure and review it regularly. If you want to improve your diet and nutrition, you will first want to write down what you eat and drink each day.

Often, awareness itself will result in a good amount of progress. Once everything is on paper, and out there under light, you cannot help but stop doing some of the bad choices you were doing, but were not aware of until now.

❖ **Start small with microactions.**

Once you become aware of current situation, most people tend to go all out on a change. Like, someone becomes aware that he is eating too much fast food but not enough raw fruit and vegetables, and they decide to go raw vegan cold turkey. That kind of sudden change is too hard to continue for most people. Therefore, most people fail at it and then totally give up on improving their diet.

Therefore, it is better to start with small changes at first. To eat less fast food, and more fresh fruit and vegetables, you could eat an apple a day before anything else. This kind of small actions are more easy to achieve. And soon, you will find that you can now take bigger actions comfortably, without any stress.

❖ **Persist for one month.**

Habits do not happen overnight. It is important to persist at least for a month. Then it will become a habit, and you will do it without any effort or thought.

And as you develop more and more good habits, you will become more successful in every area of your life.

CH. 3 THE BEST PERSONAL HABITS

We all have our own habits, our own way of doing things and that commitment to a routine is important. It enables us to function at certain times on auto-pilot and not have to fully concentrate and engage. Driving a familiar route, early morning routines, regular work related tasks are classic examples of this mindset. But it is also important to have times when we are not too rigid in our approach, are receptive to changing old, unhelpful habits and are open to a more positive way of doing things.

Let's look at some of the best personal habits to have.

- ✓ Being clean and tidy makes a difference to how we feel about ourselves and how others receive us. It indicates that we are proud of ourselves and the image we convey. It also shows respect for the people we mix with, our friends, family and co-workers. This does not necessarily mean always wearing our best clothes and make-up. It does mean that we care enough to have good hygiene, shower, maybe shave, brush our teeth, wear clean clothes. We are prepared to make an effort to dress nicely on occasion.

✓ Taking time for ourselves is an important personal habit. It is a good way to manage stress and indicates that we value ourselves. Getting into the habit of having quality 'me' time is important. Even if it is only twenty minutes sitting outside with a cup of tea, listening to music, or reading a book, taking time for ourselves is a good personal habit to adopt.

✓ Time spent with family is an important habit. Eating together regularly is a good routine as family get into the habit of talking, sharing stories about their day, and as such maintain their relationships with each other. This is a way for family to notice early on if one member is unhappy or has changes in their behaviour. It flags up problems sooner rather than later.

✓ Good food related habits are important. It can become all too easy to live off snacks throughout the day but this can result in a person's appetite becoming erratic. People who snack sometimes find that they are not hungry at meal times and end up living off junk food, crisps, sweets, biscuits. Equally, ready-made meals can seem the simple option for busy people, but taking the time to perhaps batch cook at weekends for the week ahead, or prepare the meal on arrival home and then do other things whilst dinner is cooking can be a good, healthier habit to get into.

✓ Exercise is one habit that gets a lot of publicity in the media, and apart from the health advantages it can also be a lovely way for a family to spend time together, perhaps at weekends or whilst the evening meal is cooking. Going for a walk or playing sport together can enhance the family bond. Single people can use exercise as a way of meeting new people and improving their social life. Joining an exercise class can open up opportunities to chat with other people, maybe share a coffee afterwards and start to build new relationships.

✓ Sleep habits can become a problem when people go to bed and prepare to not sleep. Taking work, books, food, television to bed changes bedtime to something other than sleep time. It can be a good habit to keep the bedroom as a comfortable relaxing place, designated for sleeping. Keeping to a regular bedtime and being aware of starting to relax an hour or so before bed helps to wind down and commit to preparing for sleep as the day draws to an end.

Setting in place good personal habits demonstrates a positive commitment to ourselves, our general health and our well-being. Good habits are often easier to maintain than bad habits once they are in place. And they support our lives, helping us to manage our stress levels in the most constructive way.

We all have habits. Some are good, healthy habits, while others are bad and possibly even dangerous. Throughout our lives we often set goals to try to create new, good habits or to break the bad ones we already possess. Many people try again and again to change their habits for the better only to meet with failure in the end. Learning a new habit can be just as difficult as breaking a bad one that you've struggled with for years. There are reasons for this and steps that you can take to help ensure your success.

Establishing good, healthy habits can enrich your life in countless ways. When an action becomes a habit, it becomes automatic and you don't really have to give it much thought.

Some of the healthy habits that people try to develop include; eating healthier, exercising regularly, meditating, completing chores around the home, or simply taking time out daily for them-selves. These are just a few examples but, basically anything that you want to do on a regular basis that will enrich your life and make you happier can become a habit.

Simple tips that are easy to follow and can help you to turn healthy activities into lifelong habits.

1. Take baby steps. - You cannot expect to just dive in and be successful when developing a good habit. Start with small manageable steps. If you would like to make healthy eating a habit, start by swapping out specific foods or meals for healthier options. If you make sudden, drastic changes to your lifestyle, the odds are good that you will not be successful.

2. Make yourself accountable. - Tell a friend or family member whose opinions matter to you. By telling a trusted friend or family member about your intension to develop a new habit you promote accountability. You will be more likely to stick to your habit if you know that you will have to answer to someone other than yourself.

3. Treat yourself. - You should be proud of the fact that you are trying to make positive changes in your life. Reward yourself regularly when you stick to your new habit. Treat yourself to a pedicure or a warm bubble bath. Spend a Saturday morning sleeping in, or play a few rounds of golf on the course. Whatever it is that you love... do it.

4. One habit at a time. - Work on developing one habit at a time. If you are anything like me, there are a ton of new, healthy habits that you want to incorporate into your life. Focus on one at a time so that you don't get overwhelmed. Developing a habit, like exercising regularly might seem like a small change but it's not. When you begin to develop a new habit of any kind you are changing the way that you live your life.

5. Make sure that you really want it. - The more you want to make even small changes, the more likely you will stick with them. Don't ever begin to develop a habit that you don't want just because you think, or have been told, that it's the right thing to do. If you try to force yourself to do something you hate, you will avoid it at all costs. If you hate going to the gym, don't do it. There are plenty of good habits that you can develop that will enrich your life and that you will enjoy.

6. Plan it out.- Sit down and make a list of the good habits you would like to develop. Prioritize the list and determine what habits you would like to develop first. Once you have this figured out, write out a plan. By putting this in writing you can refer back to it whenever you need a bit of extra motivation and it will help you stay on track.

7. Be very specific. - Don't just say, "I want to make it a habit to drink more water". Instead, say, "I want to begin drinking eight glasses of water each day". By being specific you know exactly what you have to do to develop your new habit and will not become overwhelmed. If you are too vague, you could easily rationalize that you drank more water today than yesterday, even if it wasn't your desired eight glasses.

8. Use tools. - Utilize every resource that you have at your disposal. You can make lists, journals, charts, spreadsheets... anything that will help you to keep track of your goals. I often use sticky notes around the house. I will place reminders on walls, mirrors, the refrigerator, and anywhere else that I think they may be helpful. They may not look pretty but they help me to stay motivated.

9. Don't berate yourself for slip-us. - We all slip up from time to time. Just yesterday, I was snacking on a few potato chips while watching television. Before I knew it, the entire bag was empty! It happens to everyone. Realize this, and don't be too hard on yourself. Remind yourself of why you wanted to develop the habit in the first place, and then start again.

Why is it so difficult to break bad habits?

There are things we do on a daily, or even hourly basis that we know aren't good for us. We bite our fingernails, smoke cigarettes, make unhealthy food choices, procrastinate, lead sedentary lives, etc. Every one of us has a bad habit that we would love to break, but we often have difficulty doing so. This is because, once a habit is developed, we rarely even notice we are doing it. It becomes part of who we are. If we want to improve our lives, breaking bad habits is a wonderful place to start.

Common reasons why we often fail at breaking bad habits.

1. We expect results too quickly. - We didn't develop our bad habit in one day, and we certainly can't expect to break it in one day either. Breaking a habit takes time. We must be patient and persistent in our goals.

2. We have a low level of self-awareness. - I have been a nail biter for the majority of my life. I do it without even thinking and am usually not even aware that I have been chewing on them until I feel pain or see blood. This is because I am not always self-aware. We

often go through life on autopilot, but when we are trying to break a habit, we need to slow down and pay attention to everything we are doing. We must make an attempt to really live in the moment. If we develop a stronger sense of self-awareness, we can head off our bad habits as soon as we begin doing them.

3. We use our habits as an emotional crutch. - Many of our habits, like smoking or turning to food when we are in need of comfort, serve as a coping mechanism for emotional stress or pain. We need to look for other, healthier substitutes for these habits. When I was trying to quit smoking, I would often exercise whenever I would feel an urge. The exercise took my mind off of my immediate craving and helped me to relieve my stress in a healthy way.

4. We don't tell anyone we are trying to break our habit. - Breaking a bad habit is extremely difficult. It is even more difficult when we do not have the support of our friends and family. We often fail to tell them out of fear. We think that by not telling them, we can avoid disappointing them if we fail. In order to successfully break a bad habit, we must tell those we love and trust. They will give us the support we need and they will also make us accountable for our actions.

5. We are too hard on ourselves when we slip back into old patterns. - Just as developing new habits is hard, breaking old ones is extremely difficult. We will all slip up from time to time. We must stay positive and remember why we want to break our habits. Do you want to be a better role model for your children? Do you want to avoid a second heart attack? Do you want your nails to be beautiful for your wedding day? Whatever your motivation is, remember, there is a very good reason why you decided to break your bad habit in the first place. When we slip up and fall back into our bad patterns, we must take a moment to remember why it is important to break the habit. Then, we must start again.

CH. 4 BEST WAYS TO MEET NEW PEOPLE AND INCREASE YOUR SOCIAL CIRCLE

If you want to meet new people outside of your existing social circle, you aren't alone. While it's great to spend time with friends and family, many people find themselves in a perpetual routine consisting of work, gym, happy hour, groceries, and movies. This can be a problem if you are looking to make new friends, start dating, or increase your social circle.

A popular option for meeting members of the opposite sex is to go out to bars and clubs at night. The biggest issue here is that such environments can be loud, dark, and are only suitable for those attracted to drinking, smoking and late nights.

There's a much better way to meet people. And this, ironically, is when you are focused on your life, not other people. Meeting people, instead of being the end in itself, becomes a natural consequence of whatever you are doing as you work on improving your life. When you focus on growing and becoming a more interesting person, you naturally meet people who are attracted to your determination and admire your ever-expanding horizons.

It's also much easier to meet other like-minded people when you are working on yourself because you are having fun, relaxed, and are at home in your surroundings. Here are the three best ways to meet people:

1. Develop Your Interests

Do you have a hobby that you can't stop thinking about night and day? Maybe it's that golf swing you're trying to master, or that fancy dance move you work on in the elevator when nobody is watching. Perhaps you just love cooking and your shelves are filled with recipes that family oooh and ahhh over.

Whatever your passions are, commit to developing your skills and hobbies further. Push yourself to be as good as you can, out of the hobbyist/amateur status into professional amateur, where you are good enough to teach others. Join a meetup group to share tips and techniques with each other. Go to dance parties or practices in your city. Try out as many golf courses and driving ranges as you can.

If possible, try to spend at least 10 hours on your interests each week. Take as many group and private lessons as you can on your passions. Read every book and article you can get your hands on. You will make remarkable progress, and naturally make friends and meet lots of people when you interact with others that you see over and over again.

2. Do Something You Care About

If you don't have a hobby, you certainly have convictions and beliefs. What do you care about? Perhaps you cherish water as a natural resource, and want to educate the public on good water habits. Or, you want to save the earth, and recycle everything you can find. Maybe you are fascinated with how blood donations work.

Whatever it is you care about, get involved. Join others in your community to organize events and activities together. Volunteer at your local blood drives. Visit your schools and libraries with your group and show pictures, books and videos of the importance of recycling or saving water.

Read your newspapers or community boards regularly for possible venues to go to. Spend as much time as you can be helping others while serving a greater purpose. You will feel good about yourself and the impact you are making, and meet many others who respect and admire your service in the process.

3. Work In Public Places

Work can be one of the best ways to meet people, especially if you are constantly meeting new and different people at various public places. Think about it. If you spend 8 hours a day working at new and different people out and about, you could easily meet 10-20 new people a day, or 50-100 people a week. That's a LOT of people. It isn't a stretch to meet 2,000-5,000 new people a YEAR, as I have done for many years.

It's said that a celebrity meets more people in a year than an average person meets in their entire lifetime. This can be very hard to imagine until you experience this for yourself. The more people you meet, the more likely it is that you'll meet people who share your interests, or others who are romantically attracted to you.

There's a great variety of jobs and public places where you could meet people. Some are less preferred; some are more desirable. The ideal job is one that allows you to meet people in a flexible way, without restricting you to work at the same place from day to day. Remember, your job should leverage your skills and talents so that your work is a natural expression of who you are. Otherwise you are getting a job just for meeting people, which isn't the best use of your time, as we've discussed. The internet is a great place to start looking for such jobs.

You may notice that the key to meeting people with ease boils down to doing what you love. When you do what you love, you feel good about yourself. When you feel good about yourself, you won't take anything too seriously, and other people will feel comfortable around you. When others are comfortable being with you, any potential friendships or romance will have a healthy foundation to bloom from.

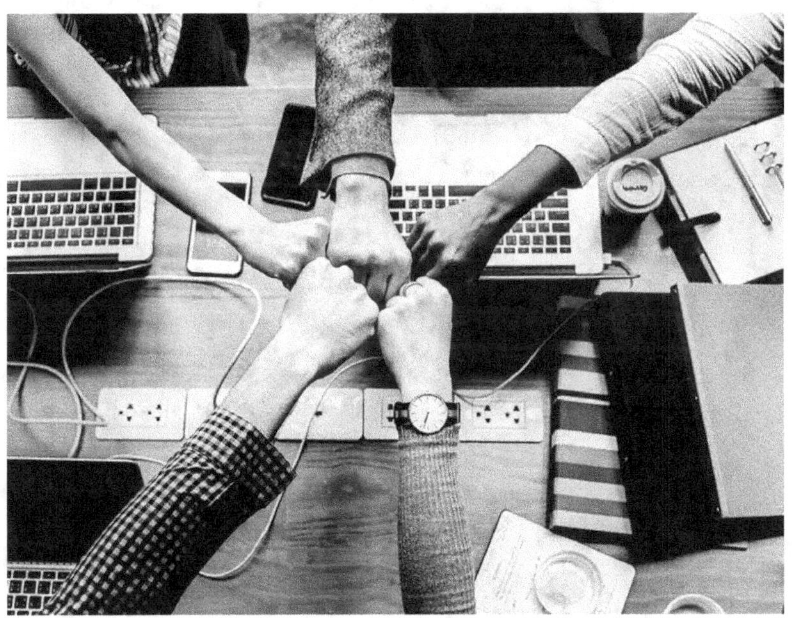

CH. 5 SLEEP HYGIENE - THE KEY TO A GOOD NIGHTS SLEEP

Good sleep habits are the things that you can do to give yourself the best chance of a good night's sleep so that you wake feeling refreshed and energized. Sleep is so important to our minds and bodies as sleep deprivation can lead to fatigue, difficulties in concentrating and learning and accidents. If you are having trouble sleeping because of stress, pain, illness or drugs then it is important to see your doctor so that the cause can be treated.

If you can't sleep and medical problems have been ruled out by your doctor; try some of these simple things which should help:

- Go to bed at the same time each night

Your natural body clock will make you feel tired when you're ready for bed. Try not to ignore your body clock; it knows when the body needs rest and recharging. Going to bed too early will result in you lying in bed not being able to sleep.

- Get up at the same time each morning

We all like a sleep in or late night occasionally and this is fine, but generally it is better to get up at the same time each morning as your body will become accustomed to sleeping and waking at regular times.

- Get regular exercise

Regular exercise improves restful sleep so try to exercise every day if possible.

- Make your bedroom restful

You stand a much better chance of a good night's sleep if your bedroom is peaceful. Keep the temperature comfortable and noise and outside light to a minimum.

- Keep the bedroom for sleeping and sex

Many people use their bedrooms for watching TV, reading, studying etc. To ensure good sleep habits it is best to avoid other activities and make sure that the bed is associated with sleeping.

- Medications

If you are taking medications be very careful to follow the directions and take them as prescribed. Many medications can alter sleep habits so don't change the times that you take them.

- Do not drink caffeine containing drinks late in the evening

Caffeine is a stimulant and can affect sleep so it is best to avoid drinks that contain caffeine in the hours leading up to bed. If you enjoy a hot drink in the evening, try warm milk, or one of the caffeine free substitutes that are available in grocery stores.

- Do not take naps in the evening

Try not to nap in the armchair in front of the TV in the evenings as this can affect the body's need to fall asleep in bed. If you are tired early evening and it's too early for bed, try to do something that will stop you nodding off, for example reading.

- Do not engage in exercise or stimulating activities before bed

Physical exercise or a stimulating activity such watching an exciting movie can stimulate the mind and you will find it difficult to switch off and wind down.

Essentials Factors for a Good Night Sleep

When the clock strikes at 5:00 pm, all you want to do is hurry home after a busy and tiring day. The first thing that would come to any one's mind is lie down on their bed and take a nap. Sleeping helps our body gain back the energy we lost after a long day's work. At the same time, it is the best way to relax both our body and mind. Having a good night sleep is not as easy as it may sound. You need to consider some factors that will help you have a relaxing and a really good sleep.

1. Noise Level. Some people can sleep even with so many noises around them, while others cannot even feel drowsy with just the sound coming from the electric fan. In order to have the sleep you want, avoid too

much noise pollution (although it depends on the person). Soft or mellow music can help the body optimize the relaxing environment it needs. It could rejuvenate our hormones and leave our mind in peace. Usually, instrumental music with light tunes and melody are advisable so as not to wake us up in the middle of the night.

2. Lighting. Turning off the light or leaving it on depends on the person's preference. There are those who prefer to sleep while the light is on. The reason behind this is maybe because they're too afraid of the dark, especially with ages between 2-7 years old when the imagination can get a little bit wild. However, it is advisable to turn off the light when sleeping, because the light can trigger our hormones that keep us awake. And besides, when you are in bed, it should connote for sleeping time and any light present can tell otherwise.

3. Room Temperature. It is important to leave your room in a cool temperature, neither too warm nor too cold. Cool room can help your body relax and rest a little better. Also it could give us a better sleeping habit. It will make you feel comfortable if the humid is right in

your bedroom. Too warm can make you feel unease and therefore disturb you in having a good night sleep.

4. Bed Condition. When choosing your bed to sleep on, it has to be comfy and could invite you to lie down at the moment you see it. Make sure that your bed sheets and bed covers are clean, as well as your pillows. Also, it should make your back and muscles relax while lying down. Avoid too crowded bed, if possible choose a king size bed where you can toss and turn around without any worries.

5. Sleep Hygiene. Last but certainly not the least, before going to bed, you should make sure that your body is really conditioned in sleeping. Being too excited or too happy can make your sleeping a little difficult. While being too tired can leave you awake for just a second. Make sure that your bed room really is just for sleeping. Avoid putting television or book shelves so as not to invite you in other task just before you go to bed.

The fact is we spend one-third of our life sleeping. Above examples are simple and common sleeping factors that are so important. Spending some time planning about your everyday sleep, will save your time and make sure you have the best rest for next day's challenges. Sleep Perfect!

CH. 6 EATING WELL AND MAKING GOOD MEAL CHOICES

Seems easy enough to make the right food choices, but those choices are not always the ones that sound the best. More and more people in our country have weight issues and there are different reasons why this is happening, though some are debatable. In any event, families are struggling with weight issues and with income issues, which makes the trouble worse. Eating healthy habits should be learned early in life so that they stick, but that does not mean you can not learn better choices for yourself and your children as they get older. Think of it as adding a lot of time and excellence to theirs.

Eating healthy habits start when a kid is very little if you begin by ice cream, candy, and other fatty and calorie ridden foods, they are going to learn to love those, and those are what they are going to want. You can not keep them from knowing about these foods forever, but if you never offer them in your home, they are going to grow to love what you do offer. Begin with vegetables, fruits and lean meats. Remember, however, that children under two need fats in their diet so go with full fat milk and some other healthy fat sources. Don't feed them junk and they won't crave it.

At what time your brood enter school, they are going to see things that you may not have wanted them to consume. You can give healthy snacks and hope that they make good choices for lunch, but you can not always know that this is true. Children can take their lunches to school, but that does not indicate they are not going to deal with others for something else. Your first-rate eating healthy practice should carry them through some, and your continued attention to helping them make good choices should keep them on the straight and narrow, though they are going to take the sweets every now and then.

Eating healthy behavior has to be accompanied by exercise and action. You do not want to line your children up and have them do jumping jacks each day, unless of course, you can make a fun, family game out of it. Instead, get everyone in the residence moving by coming up with family activities like bicycling, mountain climbing, and playing at the park. If your children are on the go, those occasional bad choices are not going to hurt them very much. They will simply work those calories off. Insist they eat well, but know that with exercise, they are going to be much at an advantage even when they opt for a cheeseburger rather than an apple when out with acquaintances for the afternoon.

It may be tricky to mature eating healthy habits when the foods that are good for you seem to be more pricey. It is easier and cheaper to get a box of macaroni than to get low fat whole wheat pastas and low fat cheeses and milk to make your own. Think of good food as medicine that will enable you and yours to live longer. They are a prescription that can guard against cardiovascular disease, stroke, heaviness, and diabetes, just to name a few. There are always ways to get those foods as they are more important than you may think.

CH. 7 HOW TO DEVELOP GOOD HABITS FOR EVER

How to develop good habits? Do you want to start a new ritual, but don't know if it is going to last? Perhaps you want to change something in your life? Perhaps you want to start sleeping early and get up early?

Whatever habit you want to develop, whether it is a new language that you want to learn, watch your diet, overcome shyness, or stop procrastinating, there are steps that will help accomplish just that. To say you want to develop a new habit is easy, but to stay committed to it is what you have to work on.

To develop good habits forever, follow the below steps:

❖ **Commit for 30 days**

Once you commit to developing and doing a new ritual for around a month, then it will become ingrained in you and it will be easy for you to maintain. Repetition is crucial, so the good habits and rituals become second nature.

❖ **Begin taking small steps**

Don't try to radically change your life. It is very easy to want to change your life all at once, but it is not realistic. If you want to start reading for two hours daily, you can start by reading for half an hour, then you would increase the time slowly.

❖ Find a friend

Befriend someone who shares the same interests to help you continue with the new habit incase you decide to stop later on.

❖ Use the word "But"

One of the best ways to stop negative thoughts is by introducing the word "But." If you start saying to yourself "I can't do this ritual. It is too hard," then you need to stop and say, "But, if I keep practicing, it will get easier."

❖ Select your friends

Spend more time with people who are positive and who you admire. The more time you spend with positive people who have the same habits and rituals, the more their positive energy will affect you.

- ❖ **Change your thoughts and imagine the end result**

If you want to go back to your old and bad habit, change your thought and begin to imagine disliking the old habit. Begin to imagine the benefits you will reap when you quit the old habit.

www.ingramcontent.com/pod-product-compliance
Lightning Source LLC
Chambersburg PA
CBHW061531250726
48657CB00005B/2180